# *The* Siberian Husky

*A guide to selection, care, nutrition,*

*upbringing, training, health, breeding,*

*sports and play*

# Contents

# Foreword

The book you are holding is not intended to be a complete 'owners' manual' for the Siberian Husky. If we had tried to cover all the information available about this breed, its history and development, feeding, training, health, ailments and whatever more, this would be a book of at least 500 pages.

What we have done however, is to collect basic information to help the (future) owner of a Siberian Husky look after his or her pet responsibly. Too many people still buy a pet before really understanding what they're about to get into.

This book goes into the broad history of the Siberian Husky, the breed standard and some pros and cons of buying a Husky. You will also find essential information on feeding, initial training and an introduction into reproduction. Finally we give attention to (day-by-day) care, health and some breed-specific ailments.

Based on this information, you can buy a Siberian Husky, having thought it through carefully, and keep it as a pet in a responsible manner. Our advice, though, is not just to leave it to this small book. A properly brought-up and well-trained dog is more than just a dog. Invest a little extra in a puppy training course or an obedience course. There are also excellent books available that go deeper into certain aspects than is possible here.

The About Pets Team

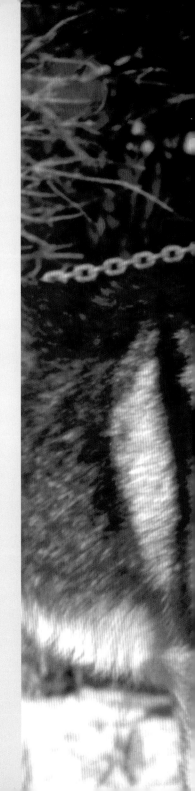

**about** pets

**A Publication of About Pets.**

Copyright © 2005
About Pets
co-publisher United Kingdom
Kingdom Books
PO9 5TL, England


ISBN 1852792302
First printed
September 2005


Original title: *de Siberian Husky*
© 2001-2005 Welzo Media Productions bv,
About Pets bv,
Warffum, the Netherlands
www.aboutpets.info

Editor: Maya Brünner

Photos:
Wilco van Dijen, Maya Brünner,
Dr. Ulrich Sobanski, Rob Doolaard and
Rob Dekker

Printed in China through Printworks Int.Ltd

# In general

**Its tolerant, well-balanced and friendly nature makes the Siberian Husky a pleasant and calm companion that is friendly towards everybody it meets. A Siberian Husky is an independent, often self-willed dog with a huge urge for exercise.**

This in-born urge for exercise is often the reason for a Husky to escape and go off on its own. It will then go out hunting, for hunting is in its blood. Whatever it hunts it will usually also kill. However obedient a Siberian Husky is at home, once it's escaped it will never obey. Therefore it's not a good idea to walk a Husky off the lead. The Siberian Husky is often called a 'trap', because owning a Husky is something quite special: a Husky can change your life. People often keep two or three. You have been warned! Your new dog will get you involved in all kinds of activities. After all, active dogs need active people.

## Character

The Siberian Husky's characteristic temperament is friendly and mild, yet lively and alert. It doesn't have the traits of a watch-dog, nor is it particularly mistrustful towards strangers or aggressive towards other dogs. An adult dog can display a certain dignity and reservedness. Its intelligence, ease of handling and willingness make it a pleasant comrade and a willing worker.

Important: The Siberian Husky needs company and a lot of exercise. You can do this dog no bigger favour than to take it on long walks, jog with it or take it on cycle rides, or any other activity where it gets lots of movement. If a Siberian Husky does not get enough attention and exercise, it will quickly get bored. It will then howl, dig up the garden, demolish your furniture or try to escape to go hunting.

### Origins

The Siberian Husky was developed by the Chuckchies, a nomadic people living in the extreme north-east of Asia. They lived in an inhospitable region of Siberia where living conditions were very tough. These nomadic tribes lived from hunting. Their dogs helped the nomads with hunting and pulling their sleds. As both these people and their dogs lived in barren conditions, a breed of dog developed that could handle a lot of work and needed little food, would remain tolerant and friendly towards each other and people under extreme conditions. Because the Chuckchies applied strict selection for these characteristics when breeding, a medium-sized, gracious, fast sled-dog developed with enormous endurance, but which always stayed tolerant, quiet, friendly and tough.

Sled dog racing started to become important in Alaska around 1900. During the 1909 All Alaskan Sweepstakes, a race over some 408 miles, the first sled dog team with dogs from Siberia took part driven by a certain Mr. Goosack. This team won third prize and made a huge impression on the population. This was not just because they won third prize, but because of the happy perseverance the team's dogs displayed. They worked with grace, yet were so robust that they earned huge admiration. Their agility, their tolerance towards each other in the team and their trust in people left a deep impression on the dog-lovers of the time. From that moment on, interest in these dogs grew in Alaska, and more and more were bought in Siberia and imported to Alaska.

In 1925, the Siberian Husky became well known outside the circle of dog lovers too. It played a key role in fighting a diphtheria epidemic. The epidemic broke out in Nome in January 1925 and the serum available there was by no means enough. It had to be fetched from far away, which at that time of year was only possible with the help of sled

dogs. In this dramatic race against death over 674 miles, which would normally need 25 days, a large number of Eskimos, Indians and trappers together with their dogs put their lives on the line. They ran in a relay.

Leonard Seppala and his dogs ran the longest, and the most dangerous, stretch. The other teams ran a maximum of 53 miles. Leonard Seppala left Nome with his team of Siberian Huskies to meet the sled dog relay. He had 316 miles behind him when he met up with the team carrying the serum in Nulato on the river Yukon. As no time could be lost, he turned around back towards Nome despite a vicious snowstorm. Although he would have liked to give his dog team some rest, his lead dog, Togo, kept the team motivated throughout and led the team back safely. As the last stage of the relay, Gunnar Kaasson and his team of Siberian Huskies led by Balto reached Nome on 2nd February 1925 with the life-saving serum. The transport had taken just one week.

Most of the names of these brave men and their dogs have long since been forgotten. But one dog serves to remind the world of this dramatic race. In memory of all the sled dogs that took part in this relay race, a statue of Balto stands in New York's Central Park.

Below it is the inscription "Endurance – Fidelity – Intelligence". This race with the serum made the Siberian Husky famous as a sled dog.

## Family members
The Siberian Husky is one of the five recognised sled dog breeds. The others are the Alaskan Malamute, the Samoyed, Greenlander and Eskimo Dog.

## Breed standard
A standard has been developed for all breeds recognised by the F.C.I. (the umbrella organisation for Western European kennel clubs). Officially approved kennel clubs in the member countries provide a translation. This standard provides a guideline for breeders and inspectors. It is something of an ideal that dogs of the breed must strive to match. With some breeds, dogs are already bred that match the ideal. Other breeds have a long way to go. There is a list of defects for each breed. These can be serious defects that disqualify the dog, and it will be excluded from breeding. Permitted defects are not serious, but do cost points in a show.

## Breed standard for the Siberian Husky

### General Appearance
Medium-sized working sled-dog, quick and light on feet. Free and graceful in action, with well

furred body, erect ears and brush tail. Proportions reflect a basic balance of power, speed and endurance, never appearing so heavy or coarse as to suggest a freighting animal, nor so light and fragile as to suggest a sprint-racing animal. Males are masculine but never coarse, bitches feminine but without weakness of structure. Muscle firm and well developed, no excess weight.

### Characteristics
Medium size, moderate bone, well balanced proportions, ease and freedom of movement, and good disposition.

### Temperament
Friendly and gentle, alert and outgoing. Does not display traits of the guard dog, not suspicious with strangers or aggressive with dogs but some measure of reserve expected in mature dog. Intelligent, tractable and eager disposition. An agreeable companion and willing worker.

### Head and Skull
Medium size in proportion to the body, presents a finely chiselled fox-like appearance. Slightly rounded on top, tapering gradually from widest point to eyes. Muzzle medium length and width, neither snipy nor coarse, tapering gradually to rounded nose. Tip of nose to stop equidistant from stop to occiput.

Stop clearly defined but not excessive. Line of the nose straight from the stop to tip. Nose black in grey, tan or black dogs; liver in copper dogs; and may be flesh-coloured in pure white. In winter, pink-streaked 'snow nose' is acceptable.

### Eyes
Almond-shaped, moderately spaced and set obliquely. Any shade of blue or brown, one of each colour, or parti-colours equally acceptable. Expression keen, but friendly, interested, even mischievous.

### Ears
Medium size, relatively close together, triangular in shape, the height slightly greater than width at base. Set high on head, strongly erect, the inner edges being quite close together at the base, when the dog is at attention

carried practically parallel. Slightly arched at the back. Thick, well furred outside and inside, tips slightly rounded.

## Mouth

Lips well pigmented, close fitting. Jaws strong, with a perfect, regular and complete scissor bite, i.e. upper teeth closely overlapping lower teeth and set square to the jaws.

## Neck

Medium length and thickness, arched and carried proudly erect when standing. When moving at a trot, extended so that the head is carried slightly forward.

## Forequarters

Shoulder blade well laid back, upper arm angles slightly backward from point of shoulder to elbow, never perpendicular to the ground. Muscle holding shoulder to rib cage firm and well-developed. Straight or loose shoulders highly undesirable. Viewed from the front, forelegs moderately spaced, parallel and straight with elbows close to the body, turning neither in nor out. Viewed from the side, pasterns slightly sloping, wrist strong but flexible. Length from elbow to ground slightly more than distance from elbows to top of withers. Bone proportionate, never heavy. Dewclaws may be removed.

## Body

Straight and strong, with level topline from withers to croup. Medium length, not cobby, nor slack from excessive length. In profile, body from point of shoulder to rear point of croup slightly longer than height from ground to top of withers. Chest deep and strong but not too broad, deepest point being just behind and level with elbows. Ribs well sprung from spine but flattened on sides to allow for freedom of action. Loins slightly arched, well muscled, taut and lean, narrower than rib cage with a slight tuck-up. Croup slopes away from spine at an angle, but never so steeply as to restrict the rearward thrust of hind legs.

## Hindquarters

Viewed from rear, hindlegs moderately spaced and parallel. Upper thighs well muscled and powerful, stifles well bent, hock joint well defined and set low to ground. Dewclaws, if any, should be removed.

## Feet

Oval, not long, turning neither in nor out in natural stance. Medium size, compact, well furred and slightly webbed between toes. Pads tough and thickly cushioned. Trimming of fur between toes and around feet permissible.

## Tail
Well furred, of round, fox brush shape set on just below level of topline and usually carried over back in graceful sickle curve when dog at attention. When carried up, tail should not curl too tightly, nor should it curl to either side of body, or snap flat against back. Hair on tail of medium length and approximately same length all round. A trailing tail is normal for dog when working or in repose.

## Gait/Movement
Smooth and seemingly effortless. Quick and light on feet, gaited on a loose lead at a moderately fast trot, exhibiting good reach in forequarters and good drive in hindquarters. When walking, legs move in parallel, but as speed increases, gradually angling inward to single track .As pad marks converge, forelegs and hindlegs carried straight with neither elbows nor stifles turning in nor out, each hindleg moving in path of foreleg on same side. Topline of back remaining firm and level during gaiting.

## Coat
Double, and medium in length, giving a well furred appearance, never so long as to obscure clean-cut outline of dog. Undercoat soft and dense; of sufficient length to support outer coat. Guard hairs of outer coat straight and somewhat smooth-lying, never harsh, rough or shaggy, too silky nor standing straight off from body. Absence of undercoat during shedding normal. No trimming of fur on any part of dog, except feet.

## Colour
All colours and markings, including white, allowed. Variety of markings on head is common, including many striking patterns not found in other breeds.

## Size
Height: dogs: 53-60 cms (21-231/2 ins) at withers; bitches: 51-56 cms (20-22 ins) at withers. Weight: dogs: 20-27 kgs (45-60 lbs); bitches: 16-23 kgs (35-50 lbs). Weight should be in proportion to height. These measurements represent the extremes in height and weight, with no preference given to either extreme. A dog should not exceed 60 cms (231/2 ins) or a bitch exceed 56 cms (22 ins).

## Faults
Any departure from the foregoing points should be considered a fault and the seriousness with which the fault should be regarded should be in exact proportion to its degree and its effect upon the health and welfare of the dog.

## Note
Male animals should have two apparently normal testicles fully descended.

January 2001

# Buying a Siberian Husky

**Once you've made that properly considered decision to buy a dog, there are several options. Should it be a puppy, an adult dog, or even an older dog? Should it be a bitch or dog, a pedigree dog or a cross?**

Of course, the question also comes up as to where to buy your dog - from a private person, a reliable breeder or an animal shelter? For you and the animal, it's vital to get these questions sorted out in advance. You want a dog that will fit your circumstances properly. With a puppy, you get a playful energetic housemate that will easily adapt to a new environment. If you want something quieter, an older dog is a good choice.

## Pros and Cons of the Siberian Husky

Before buying a Siberian Husky, you should consult with yourself and your family whether you are prepared to put up with the negative aspects that are related to keeping this breed. If you are

prepared to live with these disadvantages, you will have the most beautiful and loving dog in the world.

**Drawbacks:**
The Siberian Husky has a double coat that protects it at temperatures down to – 60°C (-76°F). This coat is exchanged twice per year, and that doesn't all happen in one day. An amazing amount of hair falls out, which can then be found everywhere, even in your coffee. A Siberian Husky is an independent, somewhat self-willed dog. It has a huge urge for exercise and loves to go out, even on its own. Especially when you're preoccupied with something, it is a master escape artist. It then goes hunting, it's in its blood.

Whatever it hunts, it will usually kill. Once it's out it will never obey you, except when it wants to. Any order to break off the hunt half way will be regarded as 'unreasonable' and ignored, however obedient it may be at home. So never let your Husky run free. A Siberian Husky is absolutely not a watchdog. These dogs are friendly towards anybody, and are certainly able to reward any burglar with a cheerful greeting. If a Husky comes towards you enthusiastically, it will greet you by licking you on the face. This is its normal greeting.

Naturally, you're now wondering if there are any advantages at all with this dog. Yes, there are more than enough, but to enjoy them you must also be able to put up with the drawbacks.

**Advantages:**
Its independence makes it a personality and a full-blown member of the family rather than an extension of it. Its urge for exercise means you can (must) go on fine long walks with it, but always on the lead. Going cycling with a Husky is ideal. A Siberian Husky has no body scent, it needs little food but of good quality. A Husky is not a watchdog and will seldom bark, so there's almost no nuisance for your neighbours. And as far as your Husky is concerned, all visitors are welcome.

## Male or female?

Whether you choose a male or a female puppy, or an adult dog or bitch, is an entirely personal decision. A male typically needs more leadership because he tends to be more dominant in nature. He will try to play boss over other dogs and, if he gets the chance, over people too. In the wild, the most dominant dog (or wolf) is always the leader of the pack. In many cases this is a male. A bitch is much more focussed on her master, she sees him as the pack leader.

A puppy test is good for defining what kind of character a young dog will develop. During a test one usually sees that a dog is more dominant than a bitch. You can often quickly recognise the bossy, the adventurous and the cautious characters. So visit the litter a couple of times early on. Try to pick a puppy that suits your own personality. A dominant dog, for instance, needs a strong hand. It will often try to see how far it can go. You must regularly make it clear who's the boss, and that it must obey all the members of the family.

When bitches are sexually mature, they will go into season. On average, a bitch is in season twice a year for about two or three weeks. This is the fertile period when she can become pregnant. Particularly in the second half of

her season, she will want to go looking for a dog to mate with. A male dog will show more masculine traits once he is sexually mature. He will make sure other dogs know what territory is his by urinating as often as possible in as many places as he can. He is also difficult to restrain if there's a bitch in season nearby. As far as normal care is concerned there is little difference between a dog and a bitch.

## Puppy or adult?

After you've made the decision for a male or female, the next question comes up. Should it be a puppy or an adult dog? Your household circumstances usually play a major role here.

Of course, it's great having a sweet little puppy in the house, but bringing up a young dog takes a lot of time. In the first year of its life it learns more than during the rest of its life. This is the period when the foundations are laid for elementary matters such as house-training, obedience and social behaviour. You must reckon with the fact that your puppy will keep you busy for a couple of hours a day, certainly in the first few months. You won't need so much time with a grown dog. It has already been brought up, but this doesn't mean it won't need correcting from time to time.

Many Siberian Huskies are still used for dog sled racing. When the dog is six or seven years old, it will slow down, and many new homes are sought for Huskies of this age. Most of these dogs have spent their lives living in kennels and have not had the upbringing that is normal for a pet dog. Despite that, a Siberian Husky will quickly adapt to its new life if it gets enough attention and exercise.

A puppy will no doubt leave a trail of destruction in its wake for the first few months. With a little bad luck, this will cost you a number of rolls of wallpaper, some good shoes and a few socks. In the worst case you'll be left with some chewed furniture. Some puppies even manage to tear curtains from their rails. With good upbringing this 'vandalism' will quickly disappear, but you won't have to worry about this if you get an older dog.

The greatest advantage of a puppy, of course, is that you can bring it up your own way. And the upbringing a dog gets (or doesn't get) is a major influence on its whole character. Finally, financial aspects may play a role in your choice. A puppy is generally (much) more expensive than an adult dog, not only in purchase price but also in 'maintenance'. A puppy needs to go to the vet's more often for the necessary vaccinations and check-ups.

Overall, bringing up a puppy costs a good deal of energy, time and money, but you have its upbringing in your own hands. An adult dog costs less money and time, but its character is already formed. You should also try to find out about the background of an adult dog. Its previous owner may have formed its character in somewhat less positive ways.

## Two dogs?

Having two or more dogs in the house is not just nice for us, but also for the animals themselves. Dogs get a lot of pleasure from company of their own kind. After all, they are pack animals and that applies especially to the Siberian Husky. A Husky can not be alone.

If you're sure that you want two young dogs, it's best not to buy them at the same time. Bringing a dog up and establishing the bond between dog and master takes time, and you need to give a lot of attention to your dog in this phase. Having two puppies in the house means you have to divide your attention between them. Apart from that, there's a danger that they will focus on one another rather than on their master. Buy the second pup when the first is (almost) an adult.

Two adult dogs can happily be brought into the home together, as long as they're used to each other. If this is not the case, then they have to go through that process. This is usually best achieved by letting them get to know each other on neutral territory. This prevents fights for territory. On neutral territory, perhaps an acquaintance's garden where neither dog has been before, both dogs are basically equal. Once they've got to know each other, you can take them both home, and they can sort out the hierarchy there amongst themselves. In any event, don't get involved in trying to 'arbitrate'. That is human, but for the dog that's at the top of the pecking order it's like having its position undone. It will only make the dog more dominant in behaviour, with all the consequences. Once the hierarchy is established, most dogs can get along fine together.

Getting a puppy when the first dog is somewhat older often has a positive effect on the older dog. The influence of the puppy almost seems to give it a second childhood. The older dog, if it's been well brought up, can help with the upbringing of the puppy. Young dogs like to imitate the behaviour of their elders. Don't forget to give both dogs the same amount of attention. Take both out alone at least once per day during the first eighteen months.

Give the older dog enough opportunity to get some peace and quiet. It won't want an enthusiastic youngster running around under its feet all the time. Moreover, a puppy needs plenty of sleep and may have to have the brakes put on it once in a while.

The combination of a male and female needs special attention and it's good advice to get a second dog of the same sex. This will avoid a lot of problems. Sterilisation and castration is, of course, one solution, but it's a final one. A sterilised or castrated animal can never reproduce.

## A dog and children

Dogs and children are a great combination. They can play together and get great pleasure out of each other's company. Moreover, children need to learn how to handle living beings; they develop respect and a sense of responsibility by caring for a dog (or other pets).

However sweet a dog is, children must understand that it is an animal and not a toy. A dog isn't comfortable when it's messed around with. It can become frightened, timid and even aggressive. So make it clear what a dog likes and what it doesn't. Look for ways the child can play with the dog, perhaps a game of hide and seek where the child hides and the dog has to find it.

Even a simple tennis ball can give enormous pleasure. Children must learn to leave a dog in peace when it doesn't want to play any more. The dog must also have its own place where it's not disturbed. Have children help with your dog's care as much as possible. A strong bond will be the result.

The arrival of a baby also means changes in the life of a dog. Before the birth you can help get the dog acquainted with the new situation. Let it sniff at the new things in the house and it will quickly accept them. When the baby has arrived involve the dog as much as possible in day-by-day events, but make sure it gets plenty of attention too. NEVER leave a dog alone with young children. Crawling infants sometimes make unexpected movements, which can easily frighten a dog. And infants are hugely curious, and may try to find out whether the tail is really fastened to the dog, or whether its eyes come out, just like they do with their cuddly toys. But a dog is a dog and it will defend itself when it feels threatened.

## Where to buy

There are various ways to acquire a dog. The decision for a puppy or an adult dog will also define for the most part where to buy your dog.

If it's to be a puppy, then you need to find a breeder with a litter. If you chose a popular breed, like the Siberian Husky, there is choice enough. But you may also face the problem that there are so many puppies on sale that have only been bred for profit's sake. You can see how many puppies are for sale by looking in the regional newspaper every Saturday. Some of these dogs have a pedigree, but many don't. Breeders often don't watch out for breed-specific illnesses and in-breeding; puppies are separated from their mother as fast as possible and are thus insufficiently socialised. Never buy a puppy that is too young, or whose mother you weren't able to see.

Fortunately there are also enough bona-fide breeders of Siberian Huskies. Try to visit a number of breeders before you actually buy your puppy. Check the parent dogs' papers to ensure they were free of hip dysplasia (HD). Ask if the breeder is prepared to help you after you've bought your puppy, and to help you find solutions for any problems that may come up.

A breeder that feels responsible for his breed will never breed with parent dogs that suffer from congenital conditions. Breeders that are members of the breed association will be struck off the list of recognised breeders if they breed with one or two parent dogs that don't meet the established standards. However there are also a lot of breeders not belonging to the breed association. These breeders do not need to follow the breeding rules and can then also breed using unhealthy parents.

Of course, a reliable breeder can also get problems with hereditary conditions within the population, but if he works according to the breed association's guidelines, then this is a guarantee for a minimum of risks. Especially when buying a Siberian Husky, which is often bred as a special dog and often also has appealing blue eyes, the importance of contacting a good and reliable breeder via the breed association can not be over-emphasised. There are also many crosses bred between the Siberian Husky and the Alaskan Malamute, which are then sold as Siberian Huskies. However, most of these dogs do not have the tolerant nature of the Siberian Husky. They are often coarse dogs lacking the supple and elegant, almost effortless, movements of the Siberian Husky.

Finally you should realise that a pedigree is nothing more or less than evidence of descent. The breed associations also award pedigrees to the offspring of dogs with congenital defects or dogs

that have never been examined for them. A pedigree thus says nothing about the health of the parent dogs.

If you're looking for an adult dog, it's best to contact the breed association, who often help place adult dogs that can no longer be kept by their owners because of personal circumstances (impulse buying, moving home, divorce etc.) or because they have become too slow for racing.

## Things to watch out for

Buying a puppy is no simple matter. You must pay attention to the following:

• Never buy a puppy on impulse, even if it is love at first sight. A dog is a living being that will need care and attention over a long period. It is not a toy that you can put away when you're done with it.
• Take a good look at the mother. Is she calm, nervous, aggressive, well cared for or neglected? The behaviour and condition of the mother is not only a sign of the quality of the breeder, but also of the puppy you're about to buy.
• Avoid buying a puppy whose mother has been kept only in a kennel. A young dog needs as many different impressions as possible in its first few months, including living in a family group. It gets used to people and possibly other pets. Kennel dogs

miss these experiences and are inadequately socialised.

## Health:

• Always ask to see the parents' papers (vaccination certificates, pedigrees, official reports on health examinations).
• Both parent dogs' hips must have been x-rayed. If both parents have an HD-negative result then everything is in order. Whenever one parent has an HD-TC rating, the other parent must be HD-negative. They must both have an official examination certificate.
• Both parents must also have had an eye examination. The official results of these examinations must not be older than one year (see the chapter Your Siberian Husky's health).
• A male dog should have a veterinary statement that he possesses two testicles fully descended into the scrotum.
• All examinations must have been carried out, and the results known, before the bitch is covered (so some nine weeks before the puppies are born).
• Never buy a puppy younger than eight weeks.
• Put all agreements with the breeder in writing. A model agreement is available from the breed association.

**Ten golden puppy rules**
1. Let your puppy out in doses: one hour's play, feeding and then three hours sleep.
2. Never let your puppy run endlessly after a ball or stick.
3. Never let your puppy romp with big, heavier dogs.
4. Never let your puppy play on a full stomach.
5. Don't give your puppy anything to drink straight after its meal.
6. Don't let your puppy run up and down stairs in its first year.
7. Don't add supplements to ready-made foods.
8. Keep an eye on your puppy's weight. Obesity can lead to bone disorders.
9. Give your puppy a quiet place to sleep.
10. Pick up your puppy carefully: one hand under the chest and the other under its hindquarters.

# Travelling

There are a few things to think about before travelling with your dog. While one dog may enjoy travelling, another may hate it. You may like holidays in far-away places, but it's questionable whether your dog will enjoy them as much.

## That very first trip

The first trip of a puppy's life is also the most nerve-wrecking. This is the trip from the breeder's to its new home. If possible, pick up your puppy in the early morning. It then has plenty of time to get used to its new surroundings. Ask the breeder not to feed the puppy that day. The young animal will be overwhelmed by all kinds of new experiences. Firstly, it's away from its mother; it's in a small room (the car) with all its different smells, noises and strange people. So there's a big chance that the puppy will be car-sick this first time, with the annoying consequence that it will remember travelling in the car as an unpleasant experience.

So it's important to make this first trip as pleasant as possible. When picking up a puppy, always take someone with you who can sit in the back seat with the puppy on his or her lap and talk to it calmly. If it's too warm for the puppy, a place on the floor at the feet of your companion is ideal. The pup will lie there relatively quietly and may even take a nap. Ask the breeder for a cloth or something else from its nest that carries a familiar scent. The puppy can lie on this in the car, and it will also help if it feels alone during the first nights at home.

If the trip home is a long one, then stop for a break (once in a while). Let your puppy roam and sniff around (on the lead!), have a little drink and, if necessary, let it do its business. Do take care to lay an old towel in the car. It can happen that the puppy, in its nervousness, may urinate or be sick. It's also good advice to give a puppy positive experiences with car journeys. Make short trips to nice places where you can walk and play with it. It can be a real nuisance if your dog doesn't like travelling in a car. After all, once in a while you will have to take it to certain places, such as the vet's or to visit friends and acquaintances.

Breeders of Siberian Huskies often take part in dog sled racing and a lot of travelling is associated with that sport. There is a good chance that a Siberian Husky puppy will already be used to travelling in a car together with the other Huskies in its pack.

## Taking your Siberian Husky on holiday

When making holiday plans, you also need to think about what you're going to do with your dog during that time. Are you taking it with you, putting it into kennels or leaving it with friends? In any event there are a number of things you need to do in good time, especially because the Siberian Husky has other habits than most other dogs. It is advisable to have a Husky accommodated in kennels where people have plenty of experience with this type of dog. In any event, you need to take care of things well in advance.

If you want to take your dog with you, you need to be sure in advance that it will be welcome at your holiday home, and what the rules there are. If you're going abroad it will need certain vaccinations and a health certificate, which normally need to be done four weeks before departure. You must also be sure that you've made all the arrangements necessary to bring your dog back home to the UK, without it needing to go into quarantine under the rabies regulations. Your vet can give you the most recent information.

If your trip is to southern Europe, ask for a treatment against ticks (you can read more about this in the Parasites chapter).

Although dog-owners usually enjoy taking their dog on holiday, you must seriously ask yourself whether the dog feels that way too.

If you're travelling by plane or ship, make sure in good time that your dog can travel with you and what rules you need to observe. You will need some time to make all the arrangements. Maybe you decide not to take your dog with you, and you then need to find somewhere for it to stay. Arrangements for a place in kennels need to be made well in advance, and there may be certain vaccinations required, which need to be given a minimum of one month before the stay.

Siberian Huskies have a thick coat and it is not good for it at all to be taken to a warm country. Days spent travelling in a car are also often not their preference, and some dogs suffer badly from car-sickness. There are good medicines for this, but it's questionable whether you're doing your dog a favour with them. If you do decide to take it with you, make regular stops at safe places during your journey, so that your dog can have a good run. Take plenty of fresh drinking water with you, as well as the food your dog is used to. Don't leave your dog in the car standing in the sun. It can quickly be overcome by the heat, with even fatal consequences. If you can't avoid it, park the car in the shade if at all possible, and leave a window open for a little fresh air. Even if you've taken these precautions, never stay away long!

If your dog can't be accommodated in the homes of relatives or friends, it might be possible to have an acquaintance stay in your house. This also needs to be arranged well in advance, as it may be difficult to find someone that can do this.

Always ensure that your dog can be traced should it run away or get lost while on holiday. A little tube with your address or a tag with home and holiday address can prevent a lot of problems.

## Moving home

Dogs generally become more attached to humans than to the house they live in. Moving home is usually not a problem for them. But it can be useful before moving to let the dog get to know its new home and the area around it.

If you can, leave your dog with relatives or friends (or in kennels) on the day of the move. The chance of it running away or getting lost is then practically non-existent. When your move is complete, you can pick your dog up and let it quietly get familiar with its new home and environment. Give it its own place in the house at once and it will quickly adapt. Always walk a different route so it quickly gets to know the neighbourhood.

Don't forget to get your new address and phone number engraved on the dog's tag. Send a change of address notice to the institution that has any chip or tattoo data. Dogs must sometimes be registered in a new community, and you must pay for a dog licence.

# Feeding

**A dog will actually eat a lot more than just meat. In the wild it would eat its prey complete with skin and fur, including the bones, stomach, and the innards with their semi-digested vegetable material.**

In this way the dog supplements its meat menu with the vitamins and minerals it needs. This is also the basis for feeding a domestic dog

## Ready-made foods

It's not easy for a layman to put together a complete menu for a dog, with all the necessary proteins, fats, vitamins and minerals in just the right proportions and quantities. Meat alone is certainly not a complete meal for a dog. It contains too little calcium. A calcium deficiency over time will lead to bone defects, and for a fast-growing puppy this can lead to serious skeletal deformities.

If you put its food together yourself, you can easily give your dog too much in terms of vitamins and minerals, which can also be bad for your dog's health. You can avoid these problems by giving it ready-made food of a good brand. These products are well-balanced and contain everything your dog needs. Supplements such as vitamin preparations are superfluous. The amount of food your dog needs depends on its weight and activity level. You can find guidelines on the packaging. Split the food into two meals per day if possible, and always ensure there's a bowl of fresh drinking water next to its food.

Give your dog the time to digest its food, don't let it outside straight after a meal. A dog should also never play on a full stomach. This can cause stomach torsion (the stomach turning over), which can be fatal for your dog.

Because the food needs of a dog depend, among other things, on its age and way of life, there are many different types of dog food available. There are "light" foods for less active dogs, "energy" foods for working dogs and "senior" foods for the older dog.

## Canned foods, mixer and dry foods

Ready-made foods available at pet shops or in the supermarket can roughly be split into canned food, mixer and dry food. Whichever form you choose, ensure that it's a complete food with all the necessary substances. You can see this on the packaging.

Most dogs love canned food. Although the better brands are composed well, they do have one disadvantage: they are soft. A dog fed only on canned food will sooner or later have problems with its teeth (plaque, paradontosis). Besides canned food, give your dog hard foods at certain times or a dog chew.

Mixer is a food consisting of chunks, dried vegetables and grains. Almost all moisture has been extracted. The advantages of mixer are that it is light and keeps well. You add a certain amount of

water and the meal is ready. A disadvantage is that it must definitely not be fed without water. Without the extra fluid, mixer will absorb the fluids present in the stomach, with serious results. Should your dog manage to get at the bag and enjoy its contents, you must immediately give it plenty to drink.

Dry chunks have also had the moisture extracted but not as much as mixer. The advantage of dry foods is that they are hard, forcing the dog to use its jaws, removing plaque and massaging the gums.

## Dog chew products

Naturally, once in a while you want to spoil your dog with something extra. Don't give it pieces of cheese or sausage as these contain too much salt and fat. There are various products available that a dog will find delicious and which are also healthy, especially for its teeth. You'll find a large range of varying quality in the pet shop.

### The butcher's left-overs

The bones of slaughtered animals have traditionally been given to the dog, and dogs are crazy about them, but they are not without risks. Pork and poultry bones are too weak. They can splinter and cause serious injury to the intestines. Beef bones are more

suitable, but they must first be cooked to kill off dangerous bacteria. Pet shops carry a range of smoked, cooked and dried abattoir residue, such as pigs' ears, bull penis, tripe sticks, oxtails, gullet, dried muscle meat, and hoof chews.

## Fresh meat

If you do want to give your dog fresh meat occasionally, never give it raw, but always boiled or roasted. Raw (or not fully cooked) pork or chicken can contain life-threatening bacteria. Chicken can be contaminated by the notorious salmonella bacteria, while pork can carry the Aujeszky virus. This disease is incurable and will quickly lead to the death of your pet.

## Buffalo or cowhide chews

Dog chews are mostly made of beef or buffalo hide. Chews are usually knotted or pressed hide. Other than these forms, a dog can enjoy little shoes, twisted sticks, lollies, balls and various other shapes; nice to look at and a nice change.

## Munchy sticks

Munchy sticks are green, yellow, red or brown coloured sticks of various thicknesses. They consist of ground buffalo hide with a number of often undefined additives. Dogs usually love them because these sticks have been dipped in the blood of slaughtered animals. The composition and quality of these between-meal treats is not always clear. Some are fine, but there have also been sticks found to contain high levels of cardboard and even paint residues. Choose a product whose ingredients are clearly described.

### Overweight?

Recent investigations have shown that many dogs are overweight. A dog usually gets too fat because of over-feeding and lack of exercise. Use of medicines or a disease is rarely the cause. Dogs that get too fat are often given too much food or too many treats between meals. Gluttony or boredom can also be a cause, and a dog often puts on weight following castration or sterilisation. Due to changes in hormone levels, it becomes less active and consumes less energy. Finally, simply too little exercise alone can lead to a dog becoming overweight.

You can use the following rule of thumb to check whether your dog is overweight: you should be able to feel its ribs, but not see them. If you can't feel its ribs then your dog is much too fat. Overweight dogs live a passive life, they play too little and tire quickly. They also suffer from all kinds of medical problems (problems in joints and heart conditions). They usually die younger too.

So it's important to make sure your dog doesn't get too fat. Always follow the guidelines on food packaging. Adapt them if your dog is less active or gets lots of snacks. Try to make sure your dog gets plenty of exercise by playing and running with it as much as you can. If your dog starts to show signs of putting on weight you can switch to a low-calorie food. If it's really too fat and reducing its food quantity doesn't help, then a special diet is the only solution.

The amounts shown on food packaging are far too much for a Husky. A Siberian Husky needs less food than another dog of comparable size. Don't give high-performance food to your Husky if you only walk or cycle with it. It only gets this type of food if it really works (pulling a sled) and

has to cover long distances, so this is not intended for a normal pet dog that just gets a lot of exercise. Don't be misled into thinking you can give your dog high-performance food and simply give it less because it does not need to perform. This is a fairy tale. A dog that gets highly nutritious food and can't work it off properly will sooner or later have problems with its digestive organs!

# Caring for your Siberian Husky

**Good (daily) care is extremely important for your dog. A well cared for dog is less likely to get sick.**

Caring for your dog is not only necessary but also a pleasure. Master and dog are giving each other some attention, and it's an excellent opportunity for a game and a cuddle.

## The coat

Caring for your dog's coat involves regular brushing and combing, together with checking for parasites such as fleas. How often a dog needs to be brushed and combed depends on the length of its coat. A Siberian Husky actually only needs to be combed intensively during the periods when its coat is changing. It moults twice a year and then loses its entire undercoat. That means a substantial amount of hair. Don't forget to also brush the undercoat out of the tail. This

is a place that is often forgotten. Your Husky needs to be brushed regularly during this period. Use the right equipment for taking care of the coat. Combs should not be too sharp and you should use a rubber or natural hairbrush. Always comb from the head back towards the tail, following the direction of the hair.

If you get a puppy used to being brushed from an early age, it will enjoy having its coat cared for. Only bathe a dog when it's really necessary. Indeed, it is not good at all to wash a Siberian Husky. It then loses much too much oil from its coat and this fat layer is intended to protect it against the influences of rain and snow. A Husky used as a real sled dog should certainly not be washed. If you do have to bathe your Husky, always use a special dog shampoo and make sure it doesn't get into the dog's eyes or ears. Rinse the suds out thoroughly. Only let your dog outdoors again when it's completely dry. Even dogs can catch colds!

A vet can prescribe special medicinal shampoos for some skin conditions. Always follow the instructions to the letter.

Good flea prevention is highly important to avoid skin and coat problems. Fleas must be treated not only on the dog itself but also in its surroundings (see the chapter Parasites). Coat problems can also occur due to an allergy to certain food substances. In such cases, a vet can prescribe a hypo-allergenic diet.

## Teeth

A dog must be able to eat properly to stay in good condition, so it needs healthy teeth. Check its teeth regularly. Get in touch with your vet if you suspect that all is not well. Regular feeds of hard dry food can help keep your dog's teeth clean and healthy. There are special dog chews on the market that help prevent plaque and help keep the animal's breath fresh.

What really helps is rto regularly brush your dog's teeth. You can use special toothbrushes for dogs,

but a finger wrapped in a small piece of gauze will also do the job. Get your dog used to having its teeth cleaned at an early age and you won't have problems.

You can even teach an older dog to have its teeth cleaned. With a dog chew as a reward it will certainly be happy.

## Nails

On a dog that regularly walks on hard surfaces, its nails usually grind themselves down. In this case there's no need to clip their nails. But it wouldn't do any harm to check their length now and again, especially on dogs that don't get out on the streets often. Using a piece of paper, you can easily see whether its nails are too long. If you can push the paper between the nail and the ground when the dog is standing, then the nail is the right length.

Nails that are too long can bother a dog. It can injure itself when scratching, so they must be kept trimmed. You can buy special nail clippers in pet shops. Be careful not to clip back too far as you could damage the skin around the nail, which can bleed profusely. If you feel unsure, have this necessary task done by a vet or an animal beauty parlour.

## Eyes

A dog's eyes should be cleaned daily. 'Sleepies' and little lumps of dried eye moisture can get into the corners of the eye. You can easily remove them by wiping them downward with your thumb. If you don't like doing that, use a piece of tissue or toilet paper.

Keeping your dog's eyes clean will take only a few seconds a day, so do it every day. If the sleepies become yellow and slimy, this points to heavy irritation or an infection. Eye drops (from your pet shop) will quickly solve this problem.

## Ears

The ears are often forgotten when caring for dogs, but they must be checked at least once a week. If its ears are very dirty or have too much wax, you must clean them. This should preferably be done with a clean cotton cloth, moistened with lukewarm water or baby oil. Cotton wool is not suitable due to the fluff it can leave behind. NEVER penetrate the ear canal with an object. If you do neglect cleaning your dog's ears there's a substantial risk of infection. A dog that is constantly scratching at its ears might be suffering from dirty ears, an ear infection or ear mites, making a visit to the vet essential.

# Bringing up your Siberian Husky

**It is very important that your dog is properly brought up and is obedient. Not only will this bring you more pleasure, but it's also nicer for your environment.**

A puppy can learn what it may and may not do by playing. Rewards and consistency are important tools in bringing up a dog. Reward it with your voice, a stroke or something tasty and it will quickly learn to obey. A puppy training course can also help you along the way.

**(Dis)obedience**
A dog that won't obey you is not just a problem for you, but also for your surroundings. It's therefore important to avoid unwanted behaviour. In fact, this is what training your dog is all about, so get started early. 'Start 'em young!' applies to dogs too. An untrained dog is not just a nuisance, but can also cause dangerous situations, running into the road, chasing joggers or

jumping at people. A dog must be trained out of this undesirable behaviour as quickly as possible. The longer you let it go on, the more difficult it will become to correct. The best thing to do is to attend a special obedience course. This won't only help to correct the dog's behaviour, but its owner also learns how to handle undesirable behaviour at home. A dog must not only obey its master during training, but at home too.

Always be consistent when training good behaviour and correcting annoying behaviour. This means a dog may always behave in a certain way, or must never behave that way. Reward it for good behaviour and never punish it after the fact for any wrongdoing. If your dog finally comes after you've been calling it a long time, then reward it. If you're angry because you had to wait so long, it may feel it's actually being punished for coming. It will probably not obey at all the next time for fear of punishment.

Try to take no notice of undesirable behaviour. Your dog will perceive your reaction (even a negative one) as a reward for this behaviour. If you need to correct the dog, then do this immediately. Use your voice or grip it by the scruff of its neck and push it to the ground. This is the way a mother dog calls her pups to order. Rewards for good behaviour are, by far, preferable to punishment; they always get a better result.

## House-training

The very first training (and one of the most important) that a dog needs is house-training. The basis for good house-training is keeping a good eye on your puppy. If you pay attention, you will notice that it will sniff a long time and do turns around a certain spot before doing its business there. Pick it up gently and place it outside, always at the same place. Reward it abundantly if it does its business there.

Another good moment for house-training is after eating or sleeping. A puppy often needs to do its business at these times. Let it

relieve itself before playing with it, otherwise it will forget to do so and you'll not reach your goal. For the first few days, take your puppy out for a walk just after it's eaten or woken up. It will quickly learn the meaning, especially if it's rewarded with a dog biscuit for a successful attempt. Of course, it's not always possible to go out after every snack or snooze. Lay newspapers at different spots in the house. Whenever the pup needs to do its business, place it on a newspaper. After some time it will start to look for a place itself. Then start to reduce the number of newspapers until there is just one left, at the front or back door. The puppy will learn to go to the door if it needs to relieve itself. Then you put it on the lead and go out with it. Finally you can remove the last newspaper. Your puppy is now house-trained.

One thing that certainly won't work is punishing an accident after the fact. A dog whose nose is rubbed in its urine or its droppings won't understand that at all. It will only get frightened of you. Rewarding works much better than punishment. An indoor kennel or cage can be a good tool to help in house-training. A puppy won't foul its own nest, so a kennel can be a good solution for the night, or during periods in the day when you can't watch it. But a kennel must not become a prison where your dog is locked up day and night.

## First exercises

The basic commands for an obedient dog are those for sit, lie down, come and stay. But a puppy should first learn its name. Use it as much as possible from the first day on followed by a friendly 'Come!'. Reward it with your voice and a stroke when it comes to you. Your puppy will quickly recognise the intention and has now learned its first command in a playful manner. Don't be too harsh with a young puppy, and don't always punish it immediately if it doesn't always react in the right way. When you call your puppy to you in this way have it come right to you. You can teach a pup to sit by holding a piece of dog biscuit above his nose and then slowly moving it backwards. The puppy's head will also move backwards until its hind legs slowly go down. At that moment you call 'Sit!'. After a few attempts, it will quickly know this nice game. Use the 'Sit!' command before you give your dog its food, put it on the lead, or before it's allowed to cross the street.

Teaching the command to lie down is similar. Instead of moving the piece of dog biscuit backwards, move it down vertically until your hand reaches the ground and then forwards. The dog will also move its forepaws forwards and lie down

on its own. At that moment call 'Lie down!' or 'Lay!'. This command is useful when you want a dog to be quiet.

Two people are needed for the 'Come!' command. One holds the dog back while the other runs away. After about fifteen metres, he stops and enthusiastically calls 'Come!'. The other person now lets the dog free, and it should obey the command at once. Again you reward it abundantly. The 'Come!' command is useful in many situations and good for safety too.

A dog learns to stay from the sitting or lying position. While its sitting or lying down, you call the command 'Stay!' and then step back one step. If the dog moves with you, quietly put it back in position, without displaying anger. If you do react angrily, you're actually punishing it for coming to you, and you'll only confuse your dog. It can't understand that coming is rewarded one time, and punished another. Once the dog stays nicely reward it abundantly. Practise this exercise with increasing distances (at first no more than one metre). The 'Stay!' command is useful when getting out of the car.

## Courses

Obedience courses to help you bring up your dog are available across the country. These courses are not just informative, but also fun for dog and master.

With a puppy, you can begin with a puppy course. This is designed to provide the basic training. A puppy that has attended such a course has learned about all kinds of things that will confront it in later life: other dogs, humans, traffic and what these mean. The puppy will also learn obedience and to follow a number of basic commands. Apart from all that, attention will be given to important subjects such as

brushing, being alone, travelling in a car, and doing its business in the right places.

The next step after a puppy course is a course for young dogs. This course repeats the basic exercises and ensures that the growing dog doesn't get into bad habits. After this, the dog can move on to an obedience course for full-grown dogs. For more information on where to find courses in your area, contact your local kennel club. You can get its address from the Kennel Club of Great Britain in

London. In some areas, the RSPCA organises obedience classes and your local branch may be able to give you information.

## Play and toys

There are various ways to play with your dog. You can romp and run with it, but also play a number of games, such as retrieving, tug-of-war, hide-and-seek and catch. A tennis ball is ideal for retrieving, you can play tug-of-war with an old sock or a special tugging rope. Start with tug-of-war only when your dog is a year old. A puppy must first get its second teeth and then they need several months to strengthen. There's a real chance of your dog's teeth becoming deformed if you start too young. You can use almost anything for a game of hide-and-seek. A frisbee is ideal for catching games. Never use too small a ball for games. It can easily get stuck in the dog's throat.

Play is extremely important. Not only does it strengthen the bond between dog and master, but it's also healthy for both. Make sure that you're the one that ends the game. Only stop when the dog has brought back the ball or frisbee, and make sure you always win the tug-of-war. This confirms your dominant position in the hierarchy. Use these toys only during play so that the dog doesn't forget their significance. When choosing a special dog toy, remember that

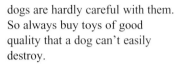

dogs are hardly careful with them. So always buy toys of good quality that a dog can't easily destroy.

Be very careful with sticks and twigs. The latter, particularly, can easily splinter. A splinter of wood in your dog's throat or intestines can cause awful problems. Throwing sticks or twigs can also be dangerous. If they stick into the ground a dog can easily run into them with an open mouth.

If you would like to do more than just play games, you can now also play sports with your dog. For people who want to do more, there are various other sporting alternatives such as flyball, agility, and obedience. There are also special tasks for dog sled racing, see the chapter Sports and shows.

## Aggression

Siberian Huskies are practically never aggressive. But even they can sometimes be difficult with other animals or people, so it's good to understand more about the background of aggression in dogs.

There are two different types of aggressive behaviour: The anxious-aggressive dog and the dominant-aggressive dog. An anxious-aggressive dog can be recognised by its pulled back ears and its low position. It will have pulled in its lips, showing its teeth. This dog is aggressive because it's

very frightened and feels cornered. It would prefer to run away, but if it can't then it will bite to defend itself. It will grab its victim anywhere it can. The attack is usually brief and, as soon as the dog can see a way to escape, it's gone. In a confrontation with other dogs, it will normally turn out as the loser. It can become even more aggressive once it's realised that people or other dogs are afraid of it. This behaviour cannot be corrected just like that. First you have to try and understand what the dog is afraid of. Professional advice is a good idea here because the wrong approach can easily make the problem worse.

The dominant-aggressive dog's body talk is different. Its ears stand up and its tail is raised and stiff. This dog will always go for its victim's arms, legs or throat. It is extremely self-assured and highly placed in the dog hierarchy. Its attack is a display of power rather than a consequence of fear. This dog needs to know who's boss. You must bring it up rigorously and with a strong hand. An obedience course can help.

A dog may also display aggressive behaviour because it's in pain. This is a natural defensive reaction. In this case try to resolve the dog's fear as far as possible. Reward him for letting you get to the painful spot. Be careful, because a dog in pain may also

bite its master! Muzzling it can help prevent problems if you have to do something that may be painful. Never punish a dog for this type of aggression!

### Fear

The source of anxious behaviour can often be traced to the first weeks of a dog's life. A shortage of new experiences during this important phase (also called the 'socialisation phase') has great influence on its later behaviour. A dog that never encountered humans, other dogs or animals during the socialisation phase will be afraid of them later. This fear is common in dogs brought up in a barn or kennel, with almost no contact with humans. As we saw, fear can lead to aggressive behaviour, so it's important that a puppy gets as many new impressions as possible in the first weeks of its life. Take it with you into town in the car or on the bus, walk it down busy streets and allow it to have plenty of contact with people, other dogs and other animals.

It's a huge task to turn an anxious, poorly socialised dog into a real pet. It will probably take an enormous amount of attention, love, patience and energy to get such an animal used to everything around it. Reward it often and give it plenty of time to adapt and, over time, it will learn to trust you and become less anxious. Try not to force anything, because that will always have the reverse effect. Here too, an obedience course can help a lot. A dog can be especially afraid of strangers. Have visitors give it something tasty as a treat. Put a can of dog cookies by the door so that your visitors can spoil your dog when they arrive. Here again, don't try to force anything. If the dog is still frightened, leave it in peace.

Dogs are often frightened in certain situations; well-known examples are thunderstorms and fireworks. In these cases try to ignore their anxious behaviour. If you react to their whimpering and whining, it's the same as rewarding it. If you ignore its fear completely, the dog will quickly learn that nothing is wrong. You can speed up this 'learning process' by rewarding its positive behaviour.

## Rewarding

Rewarding forms the basis for bringing up a dog. Rewarding good behaviour works far better than punishing bad behaviour and rewarding is also much more fun. Over time, the opinions on how to bring up for dogs have gradually changed. In the past the proper way to correct bad behaviour was regarded to be a sharp pull on the lead. Today, experts view rewards as a positive incentive to get dogs to do what we expect of them.

There are many ways to reward a dog. The usual ways are a stroke or a friendly word, even without a tasty treat to go with it. Of course, a piece of dog biscuit does wonders when you're training a puppy. Be sure you always have something delicious in your pocket to reward good behaviour. Another form of reward is play. Whenever a dog notices you have a ball in your pocket, it won't go far from your side. As soon as you've finished playing, put the ball away. This way your dog will always do its best in exchange for a game.

Despite the emphasis you put on rewarding good behaviour, a dog can sometimes be a nuisance or disobedient. You must correct such behaviour immediately. Always be consistent: once 'no' must always be 'no'.

## Barking & howling

Dogs which bark and howl too much and too often are a nuisance for their surroundings. A dog-owner may tolerate barking and howling up to a point, but neighbours are often annoyed by the unnecessary noise. Don't encourage your puppy to bark and howl. Of course, it should be able to announce its presence, but if it goes on barking it must be called to order with a strict 'Quiet!'. If a puppy fails to obey, just hold its muzzle closed with your hand.

A Siberian Husky will often howl for long periods when left alone. It feels alone and tries to get someone's attention by howling. There are special training programmes for this problem, where a dog learns that being alone is nothing to be afraid of, and that its master will always return.

You can practise this with your dog at home. Leave the room and come back in at once. Reward your dog if it stays quiet. Gradually increase the length of your absences and keep rewarding it as long as it remains quiet.

Never punish the dog if it does bark or yelp. It will never understand punishment afterwards, and this will only make the problem worse. Never go back into the room as long as your dog is barking, as it will view this as a reward. You might want to make the dog feel more comfortable by switching the radio on for company during your absence. It will eventually learn that you always come back and the barking will reduce. If you don't get the required result, attend an obedience course.

The Siberian Husky is a pack animal that can't deal with being alone. If you're out of the house all day, there's a good chance your Husky will howl. This is one reason many people keep several Huskies.

## Undesirable behaviour

The undesirable behaviour displayed by the Siberian Husky is what it gets up to simply because it is a Husky and possesses this breed's typical characteristics. You cannot change this behaviour and must simply be prepared to accept that it has these traits and you have to live with them.

1. A Siberian Husky that does not get enough exercise will look for things to keep itself busy, which may be demolishing the inside of your home or ploughing up the lawn. This is easily solved by giving your dog enough exercise. Once around the block is simply not enough for a Husky. It will rather regard a walk of 6 to 7 miles as "normal". Of course, you can always build a kennel for it where it can stay when you're out of the house.
2. Anyone that wants to keep a Siberian Husky must make sure their garden has a high enough and secure fence. A Husky is a master escape artist. There are enough examples of Huskies that manage to jump a 6-foot wall. There are also countless

examples that can climb and thus find a way to freedom. Not every Husky climbs, but this can be solved by building a kennel closed at the top.
3. The Siberian Husky is a hunter and will normally kill its prey. This might be the neighbour's cat or your children's rabbit. This instinct to hunt cannot be corrected, but if a puppy grows up with a cat, a rabbit or a similar pet, it will never harm the animals it knows. But this is no guarantee that it will leave other people's animals in peace. Its hunting instinct is often the Husky's downfall and is the reason it may be shot or locked up in an animal shelter. So never let your Husky run free. That way you save yourself, your dog and its breeder a lot of trouble.
4. A Husky is a pack animal and usually cannot deal with being alone. It will howl and can keep this up for hours on end. Your neighbours certainly won't appreciate it. So the Husky is not a dog for people that are out of the house all day. Getting a second dog can solve your Husky's loneliness.

If you have problems with your Husky, get in touch with the breeder. He is the person that can put you in touch with the right channels. After all, not all dog enthusiasts are familiar with the behavioural traits of the Siberian Husky.

# Reproductio

**Dogs, and thus Siberian Huskies, follow their instincts, and reproduction is one of nature's important processes. For people who enjoy breeding dogs this is a positive circumstance.**

Those who simply want a cosy companion however, will miss the regular adventures with females on heat and unrestrainable males like a toothache. But knowing a little about reproduction in dogs will help you to understand why they behave the way they do, and what measures you need to take when this happens.

## Liability
Breeding dogs is much more than simply 1+1= many. If you're planning to breed with your Siberian Husky, be on your guard, otherwise the whole affair can turn into a financial drama because, under the law, a breeder is liable for the 'quality' of his puppies.

The kennel clubs place strict conditions on animals used for breeding. They must be examined for possible congenital defects (see the chapter Your Siberian Husky's health). This is the breeder's first obligation, and if you breed a litter and sell the puppies without these checks having been made, you can be held liable by the new owners for any costs arising from any inherited defects. These (veterinary) costs can be enormous! So contact the breed association if you plan to breed a litter of Siberian Huskies.

## The female in season
Bitches become sexually mature at about eight to twelve months. Then they go into season for the first time. They are 'on heat' for

two to three weeks. During this period they discharge little drops of blood and they are very attractive to males. The bitch is fertile during the second half of her season, and will accept a male to mate. The best time for mating is then between the ninth and thirteenth day of her season.

A female's first season is often shorter and less severe than those that follow. If you do want to breed with your female you must allow this first (and sometimes the second) season to pass. Most bitches go into season twice per year, however Siberian Huskies often have only one season per year.

If you do plan to breed with your Siberian Husky in the future, then sterilisation is not an option to prevent unwanted offspring. A temporary solution is a contraceptive injection, although this is controversial because of side effects such as womb infections.

## Phantom pregnancy

A phantom pregnancy is a not uncommon occurrence. The female behaves as if she has a litter. She takes all kinds of things to her basket and treats them like puppies. Her milk teats swell and sometimes milk is actually produced. The female will sometimes behave aggressively towards people or other animals,

as if she is defending her young. Phantom pregnancies usually begin two months after a season and can last a number of weeks. If it happens to a bitch once, it will often then occur after every season. If she suffers under it, sterilisation is the best solution, because continual phantom pregnancies increase the risk of womb or teat conditions.

In the short term a hormone treatment is worth trying, perhaps also homeopathic medicines. Camphor spirit can give relief when teats are heavily swollen, but rubbing the teats with ice or a cold cloth (moisten and freeze) can also help relieve the pain. Feed the female less than usual, and makes sure she gets enough distraction and extra exercise. Siberian Huskies that are worked with practically never suffer from phantom pregnancies.

## Preparing to breed

If you do plan to breed a litter of puppies, you must first wait for your female to be physically and mentally full-grown. In any event you must let her first season pass. To mate a bitch, you need a male. You could simply let her out on the street and she will quickly return home pregnant. But if you have a pure-bred Siberian Husky, then it certainly makes sense to mate her with the best possible candidate, even if she has no pedigree. Proceed with caution

and think especially about the following: Accompanying a bitch through pregnancy, birth and the first eight to twelve weeks afterwards is a time consuming affair. Never breed with Siberian Huskies that have congenital defects and this also applies to dogs without papers. The same goes for hyperactive, nervous and shy dogs. If your Siberian Husky does have a pedigree, then mate her with a dog that also has one. For more information, contact the breed association.

## Pregnancy

It's often difficult to tell at first when a bitch is pregnant. Only after about four weeks can you feel the pups in her belly. She will now slowly get fatter and her behaviour will usually change. Her teats will swell during the last few weeks of pregnancy. The average pregnancy lasts 63 days, and costs her a lot of energy. In the beginning she is fed her normal amount of food, but her nutritional needs increase in jumps during the second half of the pregnancy. Give her approximately fifteen percent more food each week from the fifth week on. The mother-to-be needs extra energy and proteins during this phase of her pregnancy. During the last weeks you can give her a concentrated food, rich in energy, such as dry puppy food. Divide this into several small portions per day,

because she can no longer deal with large portions of food. Towards the end of the pregnancy, her energy needs can easily be one-and-a-half times more than usual.

After about seven weeks the mother will start to demonstrate nesting behaviour and to look for a place to give birth to her young. This might be her own basket or a special birthing box. This must be ready at least a week before the birth to give the mother time to get used to it. The basket or box should preferably be in a quiet place.

## The birth

The average litter is between three and nine puppies. The birth usually passes without problems. Of course, you must contact your vet immediately if you suspect a problem!

## Suckling

After birth, the mother starts to produce milk. The suckling period is very demanding. During the first three to four weeks the pups rely entirely on their mother's milk. During this time she needs extra food and fluids. This can be up to three or four times the normal amount. If she's producing too little milk, you can give both mother and her young special puppy milk. Here too, divide the high quantity of food the mother needs over several smaller portions. Again, choose a concentrated, high-energy, food and give her plenty of fresh drinking water, but not cow's milk, which can cause diarrhoea.

You can give the puppies some supplemental solid food when they are three to four weeks old. There are special puppy foods available that follow on well from the mother's milk and can easily be eaten with their milk teeth.

Ideally, the puppies are fully weaned, at an age of six or seven weeks, i.e. they no longer drink their mother's milk. The mother's milk production gradually stops and her food needs also drop. Within a couple of weeks after weaning, the mother should again be getting the same amount of food as before the pregnancy.

### Castration and sterilisation

As soon as you are sure your bitch should never bear a (new) litter, a vasectomy or sterilisation is the best solution. During sterilisation (in fact this is normal castration) the uterus, and often the ovaries, is removed in an operation. The bitch no longer goes into season and can never become pregnant. The best age for a sterilisation is about eighteen months, when the bitch is more or less fully grown.

A male dog is usually only castrated for medical reasons or to correct undesirable sexual behaviour. During a castration the testicles are removed, which is a simple procedure and usually without complications. There is no special age for castration but, where possible, wait until the dog is fully grown. Vasectomy is sufficient where it's only a case of making the dog infertile. In this case the dog keeps its sexual drive but can no longer reproduce.

# Sports and shows

**Siberian Huskies are active dogs that will not be satisfied with the occasional short stroll. They will quickly get bored and will misbehave at home. If you want to keep your Husky happy then you need to be active with it. An active dog needs an active master.**

A Siberian Husky is a real working dog that was not born to lie around. It will enjoy doing something together with its master. If you regularly participate in activities with your Husky, you will notice how the bond between master and dog strengthens, but also that your dog becomes quieter and more obedient. You will be amazed by everything you can do with your Husky and this chapter will give you an idea of the various options. The breed association will be happy to help you further.

### Important!

Whatever you do with your Husky, always use good sense. The Siberian Husky is a polar dog and will seldom, if ever, put in much effort at temperatures above 15° C (59°F). This does not mean walking or even running with you, but rather running beside your cycle or work needing physical effort. If it does have to work at these temperatures, it can quickly suffer from heat-stroke, which can be fatal. The dog sled working season is from September until March or April. They have a rest period during the summer and things are less active. The best time to be active with your Husky is first thing in the morning or late at night.

### Sled dog sports

This sport is even possible for people with just one or two Huskies. You must teach them to turn right (gee) and left (haw) on command, otherwise they cannot be steered. There are various types of sled dog sports:

## Skijoring

Here the dog wears a harness connected by an elastic line to a belt worn by its master. The intention is that the master tries to run as fast as possible. The human factor usually provides the braking effect in this sport as the dog can usually run much faster than its master. The combination (master and dog) with the fastest time wins in competition.

## Scandinavian pulka racing

This is based on skijoring, and comes into its own for longer distances and if you want the dog to really pull. The dog again wears a harness and is attached to a yoke between two light shafts. Behind these shafts is a very small sled carrying a certain weight. The dog pulls this sled and its master is connected to the sled by an elastic line and tries to run as fast as possible. Naturally, the combination with the fastest time again wins first prize. This is the most athletic form of sled dog sport. Both dog and master must perform.

At every sled dog competition, there are always these two classes for people with one or two dogs. The dog must possess a pedigree to participate in these competitions.

## Cycling and running

Dog sports don't only mean the dog must perform, but its master too. This is the appeal of dog sports: being busy together.

## Cycling with a springer

This is the safest way to go cycling with your dog. Your dog is attached to a bar which is in turn attached to the cycle frame. You have both hands on the handlebars, which is certainly not a superfluous luxury with a Siberian Husky. People holding their Husky's lead in their hands are often pulled off a cycle because their dog sees something it wants to chase. It won't succeed quite as quickly in a springer.

Springer

## Cycling pulled by dogs

Here, a special bar is fitted to the cycle frame and one or two Siberian Huskies are connected to the cycle by means of a towing rope. This has already become a sled dog sports class in Germany. This is actually the place to start for people with one or two sled dogs. Your dogs must obey the commands for 'Gee', 'Haw' and so on otherwise they can't be steered. For your own safety, set the cycle's saddle so low that you can reach the ground with both feet. The cycle should also be equipped with very good drum brakes.

## Cycling holiday

If temperatures are not too high, this is an ideal way to go on holiday. One can take a trailer where the dog can rest if it becomes too warm.

## Short holiday tour with bivouac

Here you go with your dogs before a cycle, scooter, or dogcart on a

Pulka

Pedal scooter

Cycling

tour, staying over night in a small tent somewhere in the woods. The next day you return via a different route.

### Run-Bike-Run
This is a combination of running and cycling organised by various societies across the country

### Triathlon with your dog
Here you go running, cycling and swimming with your dog.

### Pedal scooter
Anything you can do with a bike, you can also do with a scooter. You don't use a normal pedal scooter but one that has been specially designed for sled dog sports. There is a bar fixed to the frame to which the dogs are connected. Apart from that there is a wide foot board, because one needs to stand firmly on the board, especially at the beginning of the run. The scooter should also have good brakes to reduce the risk of accidents. Here too, the dog must be able to understand your commands.

### Full and half-marathons
There are athletics clubs where you can train together with your dog. Anyone that runs marathons can also do this with his Siberian Husky. Make sure the temperature doesn't go over 15°C (59°F), otherwise it's too hot for your Husky.

### Sacco dogcart
This is a small cart the master sits on. Before it are one or two bars with a yoke, therefore for one or two dogs. The dogs are spanned between the bars wearing a special harness here too, by which they are attached to the bars. The dogs are steered by means of the bars. This is done by applying pressure on the right side of the dog with the bar when it should turn left and on the left side to go right. If you call the relevant command at the same time, your dog will eventually learn which way to go. These carts are ideal for training lead dogs. Anyone owning a Siberian Husky can go on trips in their surroundings with a Sacco dogcart or take part in tours.

### Long distance hiking
Here the possibilities are endless. A Siberian Husky loves nothing more than walking, and many owners have unwillingly become long-distance hikers.

### Overnight hikes
In many areas, overnight camping hikes are organised. Baggage is transported to the campsite. You only carry what you and your dog need enroute. In the evenings, there's a campfire and you sleep in tents.

### Backpacking
These are hikes where both the dog and master carry a rucksack. There are whole-day hikes, or even hikes of several days.

## Four-day walks

As the name suggests, you walk four days with your own dog. Generally a lot of other people and their dogs walk with you.

## Hut tours

These tours are usually carried out in mountainous areas. These are hikes of a week or more and you walk as you want from hut to hut, staying over night in a hut. Before you go, you need to make sure you can take your dog into the hut.

## Mountain hiking

These are hikes, or even climbs, in high mountains. Here too there are tours in stages, you can hike or climb from mountain to mountain. This depends on how fit and experienced you are. These hikes come in all categories, from easy to very difficult. You take your own overnight gear with you, but sometimes you can staying over night in huts. Never take on a hike that is too difficult as this entails a high risk and you won't experience it as a pleasure.

The dogs can handle these tours effortlessly and they enjoy them.

## Survival tours

Yes, there are even special survival tours for man and dog. You can't imagine how crazy these are but your Siberian Husky will love it.

## Winter sports activities

Huskies are extremely suitable for winter sports.

## Skijoring

In the snow, this is something completely different. Skis replace shoes. The elastic line to the belt stays. This makes it especially difficult for anybody not experienced with long skis. The dog wants to run ahead and its master must learn how to cover the terrain on skis.

## Scandinavian pulka

Here too, the shoes are replaced by skis. The small cart is replaced by the pulka, a boat-shaped sled with weight in it. Naturally, the fastest time wins again.

Backpacking

Dogcart

## Sprint sled

A proud owner of two Siberian Huskies can span both his dogs before a small, light sled and try out steering it.

## On snowshoes

Here you go walking on fresh snow in snowshoes, connected to your Siberian Husky by a rope and a special belt around the waist. Snowshoes are like big tennis rackets that you attach to the soles of your shoes.

## Skating with your dog

A new phenomenon - and one condition is that you can skate very well. The most important thing is to be able to brake properly because a Husky is strong. A dog that obeys properly is even more important.

## Other sports

There are also other types of dog sport that a Husky will enjoy. But keep the Husky's character in mind.

### Agility

Agility is a dog sport where the dog must run a particular course accompanied by its master. A number of obstacles must be mastered on the way. The art is to do this with as few penalty points as possible. Many local kennel clubs organise agility competitions. The master steers his dog from obstacle to obstacle off the lead by using his voice and certain movements. A Siberian Husky is an intelligent and also fast dog. One problem is that it should never be let off the lead. If agility is carried out indoors, then there's no

problem and your Husky can take part. Huskies love taking part in agility, but if the course is outdoors there's a good chance it will take off!

**Flyball**
Flyball is another form of dog sport. The dog must jump four fences and then press on a plank with its paw. This launches a ball that the dog must retrieve and take back to its master. The dog with the fastest time wins here too.

**Behaviour and obedience**
The basis of many of the above activities is obedience, and what is very important is your contact with your dog. There is a whole range of obedience courses available, beginning with a puppy course. Even though a Husky likes to go its own way, it is possible to attend one of these courses. If you have good contact with your dog, you can go a long way here. After elementary obedience courses, you can train your dog for behaviour and obedience diplomas.

**Road safety**
Road safety courses for dogs are especially useful. Here your Siberian Husky can learn a number of obedience exercises and show that it behaves safely in traffic.

**Exhibitions and exemption shows**
Visiting a dog show is a pleasant experience for both dog and master, and for some dog-lovers it is an intensive hobby. They visit countless shows every year. Others find it nice to visit an exemption show with their dog just once. It's worth making the effort to visit an exemption show where a judge's experienced eyes will inspect your Husky and assess it for form, gait, condition and behaviour. The judge's report will teach you your dog's weak and strong points, which may help you when choosing a mate for breeding. You can also exchange experiences with other Husky owners. Official exemption shows are only open to dogs with a pedigree.

**Ring training**
If you've never been to an exemption show, you're probably tapping in the dark in terms of what will be expected of you and your dog. Many kennel clubs organise so-called ring training courses for dogs going to an exemption show for the first time. This training teaches you exactly what the judge will be looking for, and you can practise this together with your dog.

**Club matches**
Almost all kennel clubs organise club matches. You must register your dog in advance in a certain class. These meetings are usually small and friendly and are often the

first acquaintance dog and master make with a judge. This is an overwhelming experience for your dog - a lot of its contemporaries and a strange man or woman who fiddles around with it and peers into its mouth. After a few times, your dog will know exactly what's expected of it and will happily go to the next club match.

**Championship shows**

Various championship shows take place during the course of the year with different prizes. These shows are much more strictly organised than club matches. Your dog must be registered in a certain class in advance and it will then be listed in a catalogue. On the day itself, the dog is kept in a cage until its turn comes up. During the judging in the ring, it's important that you show your dog at its best. The judge gives an official verdict and issues a report. When all the dogs from that class have been judged, the best are selected. After the judging for that breed is finished, you can pick up your report and any prize you may have won. The winners of the various classes then compete for the title Best of Breed where a winner is chosen from all the dogs in the same breed group. Finally, the winners of each breed group compete for the title of Best in Show.

Of course, your dog must look very smart for the show. The judge will not be impressed if its coat is not

clean or is tangled, and if its paws are dirty. Nails must be clipped and teeth free of plaque. The dog must also be free of parasites and ailments. A bitch must not be in season and a male must be in possession of both testicles. Apart from those things, judges also hate badly brought-up, anxious or nervous dogs. Get in touch with your local dog club or the breed association if you want to know more about shows.

**Don't forget!**

If you're planning to take your dog to a club match or show, you need to be well prepared. Don't forget the following:

**For yourself:**
• Registration card
• Food and drink
• Safety pin for the catalogue number
• Chair(s)

**For your dog:**
• Food and drink bowls and food
• Dog blanket and perhaps a cushion
• Show lead
• A brush

# Parasites

All dogs are vulnerable to various sorts of parasites. Parasites are tiny creatures that live at the expense of another animal. They feed on blood, skin and other body substances. There are two main types.

Internal parasites live within their host animal's body (tapeworm and roundworm) and external parasites live on the animal's exterior, usually in its coat, such as fleas and ticks, but also in its ears (ear mite).

## Fleas

Fleas feed on a dog's blood. They cause not only itching and skin problems, but can also carry infections such as tapeworm. In large numbers they can cause anaemia and dogs can also become allergic to a flea's saliva, which can cause serious skin conditions. So it's important to treat your dog for fleas as effectively as possible, not just on the dog itself but also in its surroundings. For treatment on the animal, there are various medicines: drops for the neck and to put in its food, flea collars,

long-life sprays and flea powders. There are various sprays in pet shops that can be used to eradicate fleas in the dog's immediate surroundings. Choose a spray that kills both adult fleas and their larvae. If your dog goes in your car, you should spray that too. Fleas can also affect other pets, so you should treat those too. When spraying a room, cover any aquarium or fishbowl. If the spray reaches the water, it can be fatal for your fish!

Your vet and pet shop have a wide range of flea treatments and can advise you on the subject.

## Ticks

Ticks are small, spider-like parasites. They feed on the blood of the animal or person they've

Tapeworm

settled on. A tick looks like a tiny, grey-coloured leather bag with eight feet. When it has sucked itself full, it can easily be five to ten times its own size and is darker in colour.

Dogs usually fall victim to ticks in bushes, woods or long grass. Ticks cause not only irritation by sucking blood but can also carry a number of serious diseases. This applies especially to the Mediterranean countries, which can be infested with blood parasites. In our country these diseases are fortunately less common. But Lyme disease, which can also affect humans, has reached our shores. Your vet can prescribe a special treatment if you're planning to take your dog to southern Europe. It is important to fight ticks as effectively as possible. Check your dog regularly, especially when it's been running free in woods and bushes. It can also wear an anti-tick collar.

Removing a tick is simple using a tick pincette. Grip the tick with the pincette, as close to the dog's skin as possible and carefully pull it out. You can also grip the tick between your fingers and, using a turning movement, pull it carefully out. You must disinfect the spot where the tick had been, using iodine to prevent infection. Never soak the tick in alcohol, ether or oil. In a shock reaction the tick

may discharge the infected contents of its stomach into the dog's skin.

## Worms

Dogs can suffer from various types of worms. The most common are tapeworm and roundworm. Tapeworm causes diarrhoea and poor condition. With a tapeworm infection you can sometimes find small pieces of the worm around the dog's anus or on its bed. In this case, the dog must be wormed. You should also check your dog for fleas, which carry the tapeworm infection.

Roundworm is a condition that reoccurs regularly. Puppies are often infected by their mother's milk. Your vet has medicines to prevent this. Roundworm causes problems (particularly in younger dogs), such as diarrhoea, loss of weight and stagnated growth. In serious cases the pup becomes thin, but with a swollen belly. It may vomit and you can then see the worms in its vomit. They are spaghetti-like tendrils. A puppy must be treated regularly for worms with a worm treatment. Adult dogs should be treated every six months.

Tick

# Your Siberian Husky's health

**The space in this book is too limited to go into all the medical ups and downs of the Siberian Husky, but we do want to give you a little information about some conditions that affect this breed more often than other dogs.**

### Hip Dysplasia (HD)

Many medium-sized and large dog breeds suffer from HD. Fortunately the number of Siberian Huskies that suffer is still very limited. The breed associations hope that strict monitoring of parent animals will keep it under control. They make examinations for HD mandatory for dogs bred by their members. By means of x-ray checks, dogs are checked for HD negative, HD TC, HD light positive or HD optima forma. If the result is HD negative then the dog may be used for breeding. It is still permitted to breed if one of the parent dogs has the result HD TC, but the other parent must be HD negative. The owners of both dogs must have an official test report.

Hip dysplasia is an anomaly in the rear hip joints whereby the hip socket does not properly enclose the head of the thigh bone. This causes infections and bone tumours that are extremely painful.

Until recently, it was assumed that HD was primarily caused by genetic factors. Recent investigations, however, indicate that while genetic factors certainly play a role in terms of a dog's susceptibility to HD, it is not only determined genetically, but also depends on the extent to which the hips (especially those of a young dog) are burdened. Therefore you should not let a young dog run up and down steps too much, and should otherwise protect its joints as far as possible.

Above all for Siberian Huskies that are to be used for dog sled sports, it is inadvisable to span them at too young an age. The young dog's bones are not yet fully hardened and they wear quickly. Once they reach the age of about one year, the bones are fully hardened and you can slowly start training.

Factors such as food quality also play a role. Limit the chance of HD as far as possible by giving your dog ready-made food of a good brand, and don't add any supplements! Make sure your dog doesn't get too fat. A Siberian Husky pup should be protected from HD in its first year. Don't let it romp too much with other dogs or chase sticks and balls too wildly. These kinds of games cause the pup to make abrupt and risky movements, which can overburden its soft joints. One important but underestimated factor behind HD is the floor in your home. Parquet and tiled floors are much too slippery for a young dog. Regular slipping can cause complications that promote HD. If you have a smooth floor, it's advisable to lay blankets or old carpet in places the dog uses regularly. Let it spend lots of time in the garden as grass is a perfect surface to run on.

**Elbow Dysplasia (ED)**
Elbow Dysplasia generally appears during the first year of a

puppy's life. This condition is similar to HD, but affects the forelegs. In the worst case ED can cause lameness. An operation is then needed, which is usually successful. The measures you can take to reduce the chance of ED are the same as for HD.

## Progressive Retina Atrophy (PRA)

Progressive Retina Atrophy is an awful condition. Once it's found its way into a bloodline, PRA is difficult to eradicate. The disease is a progressive degeneration of the retina that inevitably leads to blindness. In the early stages, the dog will still be able to see well in daylight until it's about five years old, but between its fifth and ninth year the dog will become totally blind.

## Cataracts

Checks for cataracts are made at the same time as the checks for PRA. Cataracts cause a clouding of the retina. The condition can occur in young animals and is passed on by both parents. If only a part of the retina is affected cataracts need not lead to total blindness, but unfortunately this is the consequence in most cases.

## Entropion and ectropion

These are genetic conditions affecting the eyelids. With entropion the eyelids are curled inwards, with ectropion outwards. Both cause the eyelashes to lay on the eyeball causing irritation, which leads to red, watering eyes. The eyes become infected and discharge pus. This can cause serious damage to the cornea and eventually even cause blindness. Entropion and ectropion can be corrected surgically.

.

# Tips for the Siberian Husky

- Get in touch with the breed association for the address of a reliable breeder
- A puppy is good for a lot of work and a few grey hairs. Think before you start
- Make sure your puppy enjoys travelling in a car
- Never let your puppy run endlessly behind a ball or stick.
- Don't let your puppy run up and down steps in the first six months
- Always ask to see the parent dogs' papers. Hips and eyes must have been examined
- Don't buy a Siberian Husky just because of its nice blue eyes
- A Siberian Husky is a hunter and will run away. Keep that in mind
- Never buy a Husky on impulse. Think about the disadvantages of the breed

- Grooming is important for your dog's health and an important part of your relationship with your dog
- Never add supplements to ready-made foods
- A Siberian Husky is an active sled dog and likes to work. Do something with it
- Don't just fight fleas, but their larvae too
- Your Husky and winter sports – ideal
- Never buy a puppy if you weren't able to see its mother
- Hard chunks and dog chews will keep your Husky's teeth healthy
- Visit several breeders before you buy a puppy
- Make sure your dog does not get too fat. Not too much to eat and plenty of exercise is the golden rule

# Breed association

Becoming a member of a breeder club can be very useful for good advice and interesting activities. Contact the Kennel Club in case addresses or telephone numbers have changed.

## The Kennel Club

1 Clarges Street
London
W1J 8AB
UK
Tel: 0870 606 6750
Fax: 020 7518 1058
Internet:
www.the-kennelclub.org.uk/

## The Siberian Husky Club of Great Britain

The SHCGB is the biggest Siberian Husky breed club in the UK. It is a club for all those interested in the Siberian Husky, whether they are owners or not. The club holds Open and Championship shows each year. Working rallies take place over the winter months allowing owners and dogs to enjoy racing around trails. Novices are welcome (make sure to get a copy of the working rally rules from the club secretary) Novices are welcome (make sure to get a copy of the working rally rules from the club secretary) and the club also organises many more events, some for working huskies, others about showing and/or judging, and even eye testing sessions. Membership is open to all persons interested in Siberian Huskies (whether owners or not) who wish to help the Club in fulfilling its objectives for the Breed.

Penny Evans
45 Deacon Place
Middleton
Milton Keynes
Bucks
MK10 9FS
secretary@siberianhuskyclub.com

Internet:
www.siberianhuskyclub.com
0871 277 6783

**British Siberian Husky
Racing Association**
Internet: www.huskyracing.org.uk

**The Scottish Siberian Husky
Club**
Secretary
Mrs Georgia Lawrence.
94 Stafford Road, Greenock.
PA16 0TE.
E-mail: alascotia@yahoo.co.uk
01475 792592
Internet: www.scottishshc.org.uk

# The Siberian Husky

| | |
|---|---|
| FCI standard: | No. 270/02.02.1995/GB |
| FCI Classification: | Group 5 – Spitz and primitive types |
| | Section 1 – Northern sled dogs without trials |
| Origin: | U.S.A. |
| Tasks: | Sled dog |
| First standard: | 1932 (American Kennel Club) |
| Shoulder height: | Male: 53 – 60 cms (21 – 24 ins.) |
| | Bitch: 51 - 56 cms (20 – 22 ins.) |
| Weight: | Male: 21 - 27 kg (46 - 60 lbs.) |
| | Bitch: 16 - 23 kg (35 – 50 lbs.) |
| Life expectancy: | 12 - 15 years |